Do you know the seasons?

Can you name them all?

Which one is your favorite?

Winter, spring, summer, or fall?

It's cold and brisk in **winter,** but snowstorms can be nice.

Some animals still move about,

in winter's snow and ice.

Do you see the icicles
and the rabbit over there?

Do you see the animal tracks
and snow that's everywhere?

It gets warm in spring,
and songbirds come around.

Nests are full of eggs.

Roots grow underground.

Do you see the birds and flowers down below?

Do you see the raindrops helping trees to grow?

It's very hot in summer.

The rays of sun shine bright.

Insects all are buzzing.

Gardens grow just right.

Do you see the cornfield,
bees, and butterflies?

Do you see the beams of sun
shining from the skies?

In fall the leaves change colors. Some birds fly away.

The air is crisp and cool.

Wind blows through the day.

Do you see the pumpkins, and the colored leaves?

Do you see the geese that fly right by the trees?

Now you know the seasons,
and what's nice about each one.

Snowflakes fall in winter.

Corn grows in summer sun.

Songbirds chirp in spring.

Red leaves are part of fall.

Now you know the seasons.
You can name them all!

Rookie Storytime Tips

Sing a Song of Seasons is a playful introduction to the seasons of the year. As you read this book to your preschooler, pause often to allow him or her to answer the questions posed by the text. It's a great way to build visual discrimination, along with an understanding of seasonal characteristics—a key part of the preschool curriculum.

Invite your preschooler to go back and find the following. Along the way, your child will reinforce his or her knowledge of signs of the seasons.

In what season would you see eggs in a bird's nest?

In what season would you see pumpkins?

In what season would you see a snowman?

Ask your child to look outside. What season is it now? How can he or she tell?

Sing a Song of Seasons

■SCHOLASTIC

Children's Press®
A Division of Scholastic Inc.
New York Toronto London Auckland Sydney Mexico City
New Delhi Hong Kong Danbury, Connecticut

Early Childhood
Consultants:

Ellen Booth Church
Diane Ohanesian

© 2010 Scholastic Inc.

All rights reserved. Published by Children's Press, an imprint of Scholastic Inc. Published simultaneously in Canada. Printed in China.

SCHOLASTIC, CHILDREN'S PRESS, ROOKIE PRESCHOOL, and associated logos are trademarks and/or registered trademarks of Scholastic Inc.

1 2 3 4 5 6 7 8 9 10 R 19 18 17 16 15 14 13 12 11 10   62

Library of Congress Cataloging-in-Publication Data

Sing a song of seasons.
    p. cm. — (Rookie preschool)
Summary: Rhyming song lyrics ask the reader to find signs of each season in the accompanying photographs.
    ISBN-13: 978-0-531-24409-8 (lib. bdg.)   ISBN-13: 978-0-531-24584-2 (pbk.)
    ISBN-10: 0-531-24409-1 (lib. bdg.)   ISBN-10: 0-531-24584-5 (pbk.)

1. Children's songs, English—United States—Texts. [1. Seasons—Songs and music. 2. Songs.] I. Title. II. Series

PZ8.3.S6139 2010
782.42 – dc22 [E]   2009005789